Diversity, Stereotyping, Favoritism, and Nepotism in Organizations

4 Topics in 1 Book

Louis Bevoc

Published by
NutriNiche System LLC

Louis Bevoc books...simple explanations of complex subjects

Diversity in Organizations
Understanding and Improving

Louis Bevoc

Published by
NutriNiche System LLC

Louis Bevoc books...simple explanations of complex subjects

Introduction

First, diversity needs to be described. It essentially means that people are unique based on their physical traits, heritage, culture, spiritual faith, personal beliefs, and social positions. While this uniqueness is not always understood, it needs to be respected and tolerated for people to live, work, and interact together in a functional society.

In organizations, diversity is a hot topic that is increasing in importance as different kinds of people enter the workforce and organizations move into the global marketplace. Gone are the days when married White Anglo-Saxon Protestant (WASP) men ran businesses while women and minorities were steered away from higher positions in the workplace. Also gone is the thinking that disabilities and sexual preferences need to be hidden, older people are of little value despite their knowledge, and only people with money are important. While the working world is far from perfect, it has come a long way in the past 50 years.

This book examines four major types of diversity in workplaces, highlights the benefits, discusses the challenges, and offers ways to improve those challenges. The types discussed are age diversity, gender diversity, race/ethnic diversity, and religious diversity. Workplace examples are used throughout the text for better understanding.

Let's move forward by analyzing, discussing, and exemplifying different types of diversity in organizations.

Age Diversity

Age diversity is unique because every person in the organization falls into this category. Employees might not look the same, act the same, think the same, possess the same amount of money or education, or belong to the same race, culture, or religion...but they all fall somewhere on the age spectrum. The number of years separating their age creates the diversity factor.

Many organizations employ multiple generations of people. These people grew up in different time periods and did not encounter the same life experiences. That being said, they do not always share similar viewpoints.

Age diversity also affects workplace communication. Technology largely impacts the way employees interact and solve problems, but traditional methods still have value in many situations. When different ages of people work together, they shape the workplace as it moves forward.

Please consider the following concerning age diversity in organizations:

Benefits

Dissimilar viewpoints are good for organizations because they promote discussion that challenges the status quo. If employees do not question the status quo, then the organization can become stagnant with little or no growth. Younger people are assets to organizations because they challenge current methods and encourage change, while older people's knowledge and experience rationalize whether or not that change will be for the better.

Technology sparks change in virtually every organization. It makes communication faster and easier, but it can also distort the intent of the message. Workplace age differentials help determine the best ways to communicate based on an individual understanding of the situation.

Organizational example

Heather and Leroy work for an engineering design firm. Leroy has been with the company for over 25 years, and Heather started working there two years ago after she graduated from college.

These two employees are working on a project, and they have some design ideas they want to present to the customer. In the past, design ideas were always hand-delivered to customers, but Heather thinks this is an outdated way of doing business. She believes a power point presentation should be made with a link for the customer to click on to access the ideas. Leroy disagrees and believes the designs should be hand delivered to avoid the misunderstanding that can occur when nobody is present for added explanation.

After some debate, Heather and Leroy agree to develop a power point presentation. However, they will deliver that presentation in-person at the customer's business to maintain an interpersonal relationship.

In short, Heather and Leroy had dissimilar viewpoints. Heather challenged the status quo by suggesting new technology, and this changed the way business was done. However, Leroy understood the importance of interpersonal relationships, so the face-to-face contact was also maintained.

Challenges

Dissimilar viewpoints are good for generating discussion, but they also produce conflicts where people focus on position instead of principle. This can lead to arguments between people of different ages that are sometimes difficult to resolve.

In terms of technology, some older people do not want to change simply because it takes them out of their comfort zone. Along the same lines, younger employees sometimes want to change just because the technology is new.

The example involving Heather and Leroy resulted in a solution that was beneficial to the employees, customer, and organization. However, not all workplace disagreements go this well...as we will see in the following example.

Organizational example

Fernando and Eileen are attorneys at a law firm. Fernando is a 25-year-old recent law school graduate, and Eileen has been a lawyer for almost 30 years.

These two attorneys are working with a client who is suing her former employer for sexual harassment. They have some video clips from workplace cameras that they want to share with the client, and Eileen wants to hand deliver them as she has done many times in the past. Fernando thinks the personal delivery is inefficient and believes the files should be uploaded to a cloud storage site where anyone can view them. Eileen disagrees because she thinks it is better to visit the client in person to show more interest in the case. She does not see any value in the technology suggested by Fernando.

An argument between Eileen and Fernando ensues, and it starts to get heated. Fernando tells Eileen that she is a "dinosaur" who in incompetent when it comes to technology. Eileen becomes angry and tells Fernando that he has no idea how to handle clients and should not have been hired by the law firm. Both attorneys leave the room upset with each other, and they tell the partners of the firm that they cannot work together on future cases.

In short, Eileen and Fernando had dissimilar viewpoints. Fernando challenged the status quo by suggesting new technology, but ended up insulting Eileen when she did not agree with his idea. Eileen did not want to change the way she traditionally conducted business, became defensive, and insulted Fernando. Both attorneys left the room upset and decided that they could work with each other again.

Improving

In the law firm example, the problem between Eileen and Fernando could have been avoided if they had each taken the time to clarify the benefits and worked toward some type of compromise. Fernando should have indicated the simplicity of uploading a file to a cloud, the time savings involved, and the fact that many people prefer information being transferred electronically. Eileen should have explained in more detail that people appreciate personal visits, and she should have added the fact that electronic often communication needs to be clarified because it is misunderstood.

Additionally, both attorneys should have avoided any type of personal attacks. This did absolutely nothing to resolve the conflict, and it caused damage to their working relationship that might not be repairable. Personal insults are non-productive, and they lead to a negative workplace environment for everyone. This prevents organizations from attaining goals and objectives and causes people to look elsewhere for employment. Eileen and Fernando should have attacked the problem instead of the other person, and they should have avoided verbally aggressive language.

If Eileen and Fernando had clarified the benefits of their ideas, worked toward a compromise, and avoided person insults, they could have found a successful solution similar to the one reached by Heather and Leroy.

In summary, age diversity occurs in every organization with employees. It is beneficial in many ways, but it also faces challenges. The best way to overcome these challenges is to take the time to explain the thinking behind ideas or changes and avoid any type of verbally aggressive language in the process.

Gender Diversity

Traditionally, the term gender has referred to men and women. However, this has recently changed to add a third category known as transgender. For the sake of simplicity, this section will only focus on males and females.

In organizations, gender diversity refers to the representation of male and female employees in the workplace. Up until the 1960s, jobs were classified for men and women. The positions available to women were limited, and higher level management jobs were designated for men only. Times have changed since then, and the government is now involved to prevent gender bias in organizations.

Male and female employees work together to accomplish tasks and achieve organizational goals, but they have different perceptions about the jobs they perform and are not always treated equally. These factors raise questions about the importance of work/life balance and gender equality, and they complicate many workplaces since there is no "one size fits all" answer.

Please consider the following concerning gender diversity in organizations:

Benefits

Gender perceptions of jobs differ, and this is good for the organization. Different ideas lead to better problem-solving and prevent gender-specific thinking. Quite simply, men and women have different job skills, product knowledge, and personal experience that inspires creativity and helps accomplish organizational objectives.

Gender-diverse workplaces are also an asset for sales and marketing because customer bases are more diverse today than they ever were in the past. Add to that the fact that half of the potential employees are male and the other half are female...and it's rather obvious that organizations cannot disregard either gender if they want to hire the best people and be competitive with their products and services.

Based on the above arguments, gender diversity should be an important aspect of every organization's growth strategy. However, it is sometimes merely treated as a shift in personnel designed to meet government regulations.

Organizational example

Nikki and Veronica are female chemical engineers at an oil refinery. They are both very competent employees, and part of their job involves traveling with sales people to provide technical support to customers.

Nikki and Veronica are welcome at the businesses they call on because they are knowledgeable about their company's products and services, and they are genuinely concerned about the well-being of the customer's employees on a personal and professional level. Additionally, some of the customers have female purchasing agents who enjoy dealing with women due to the things they have in common and the bond they establish.

Nikki and Veronica are top-notch engineers who understand their products and customers. Upper management at the oil refinery understands the importance of these two women and realizes that diversity helps the organization grow and positivity affects the bottom line.

Challenges

One of the major issues with gender diversity is that CEOs typically do not get personally involved with its implementation and maintenance. They tend to delegate this task to specialized committees or teams so they can focus on other "more important" tasks. When this happens, the significance of gender diversity is reduced, and it gets placed on the organizational "back burner."

Another challenge is the fact that, regardless of the advancements that have been made, a "glass ceiling" still sometimes exists for females...and even for some males. Glass ceilings prevent organizations from reaching their full potential because new ideas, thoughts, and concepts are stifled.

Organizational example

Shelia is an executive at a hazardous waste removal company. She has been promoted three times during her 17-year career, and she is now being recommended for the CEO position by the CEO after he retires next month.

The board of directors realizes Sheila has done a great job for the organization. She has been in charge of several successful projects, and her cost-savings track record is one of the best in the company. However, men have always been in the top position of this company, and the board believes a male is necessary for this job because the hazardous waste industry is very male-dominated. Based on this thinking, they promote a male executive to the CEO position.

The man promoted to the position is a very competent manager, but he does not have the cost-saving background that Sheila possesses. This is a problem for the company because one of its major goals is to reduce costs by 15 percent over the next three years.

In short, Sheila does not get the CEO position due to the board of directors' thinking that the job should be filled by a man. This "glass ceiling" also prevents the organization from being its best in terms of cost-cutting because Sheila was the most qualified person for achieving that goal.

Improving

In the hazardous waste removal company example, the current CEO should have been involved in the decision-making process. He knew Sheila was the right person for the position, and that is why he recommended her. However, Instead of staying actively involved in the selection process, he left the decision up to the board of directors.

The glass ceiling also held Sheila back. The board of directors thought that the position was best suited for a man, and this sealed Sheila's fate...regardless of her qualifications. Again, involvement of the current CEO could have made a difference. He could have prevented the glass ceiling by questioning the decisions of the board members and forcing them to focus on qualifications instead of gender.

In summary, gender diversity is the equal distribution of males and females in a workplace. This balance benefits the overall health of the organization by generating new insight and ideas that positively affect the bottom line. Gender diversity also faces challenges in the form of glass ceilings and limited involvement from top decision-makers. The best way to overcome these challenges is for CEOs to be part of the implementation and maintenance of solid gender diversity programs.

Racial/Ethnic Diversity

This type of diversity is based on people and their linkages. These people include Asians, Blacks, Latinos (Hispanics), Native Americans, and Whites who are associated by their skin color, ancestry, culture, or nationality.

In organizations, racial/ethnic diversity refers to the representation of the groups mentioned above in the workplace. Similar to gender diversity, many of the best jobs in the past were only available to white people, and minorities were forced to take lower-paying positions. Once again, the government stepped in and now monitors workplaces to prevent racial/ethnic bias in organizations.

Today, people of all different colors and backgrounds work together every day in many organizations across the United States. They strive to accomplish the same objectives, but their ethnic and racial differences play a role in their perception of the workplace and the way they are treated by management. These variances lead to major debates on best business practices, and there is no universal solution.

Please consider the following concerning racial/ethnic diversity in organizations:

Benefits

Teams benefit the most from racial/ethnic diversity in organizations. The combined skills, knowledge, and cultural understanding of members create a synergy that cannot be found in homogeneous teams. Differing viewpoints contribute to overall effectiveness and improve decision-making, and this works well for complex projects that involve innovative thinking.

Racial/ethnic diversity in organizations also helps employees gain a better understanding of each other's roles in the workplace. Subconscious barriers of cultural judgment and racial intolerance are broken down as employees become more empathetic towards their coworkers.

Organizational example

Dhar and Jamie work for an international trading company that exports goods to Europe. Dhar immigrated to the United States from India, and he practices Hinduism. Jamie has been a US citizen her entire life, and she is not a member of any organized religion.

Over the past year, Dhar and Jamie have worked together on several different projects. In the beginning, Jamie would establish a position during the decision-making process and defend it vigorously. If anyone disagreed with her ideas, she would argue with them until they sided with her or the problem was resolved by someone in higher management. Dhar, on the other hand, has always followed the Hindu thinking that he must appreciate his adversary's point of view because there is no absolute truth. There are multiple solutions to the same problem, and more than one person can be right.

Dhar's behavior establishes great respect for him from other team members, and this is impressive to Jamie. After observing his actions for a while, Jamie begins to change her ways. She starts to listen to other team members' viewpoints, and this leads her to accept ideas and thinking that are different from her own.

Jamie's behavioral change greatly improves the problem-solving ability of the team. Her acceptance of other members' thoughts and ideas creates an environment of innovative thinking, and It is due to the actions of an employee from a different culture.

Challenges

One challenge associated with racial/ethnic diversity involves communication. Employees from different cultures or nationalities do not always understand each other, and this can lead to confusion and ineffective job performance.

Another issue with racial/ethnic diversity involves integration. Employees from different races or ancestries often form social groups in the workplace. These divisions develop naturally and prevent employees from leaving their comfort zones. Consequently, the cross-cultural exchange of knowledge and information is hindered because coworker relationships are limited to those with the same racial or ethnic classification.

Organizational example

D'Andre and Juan are production workers at a food processing plant. D'Andre is a Black male, and Juan is a Hispanic male. They are both good employees and have worked their way up to line leaders in the same department.

During company breaks, D'Andre sits at a table with all Black employees, and Juan sits at a different table with all Hispanic employees. This makes the breaks more enjoyable for each man due to commonality factors, but they never converse with each other or discuss ways to make their jobs easier, better, or more efficient.

Essentially, the cultural differences between D'Andre and Juan prevent them from leaving their comfort zones and exchanging knowledge. This hinders the growth of both employees and the food processor.

Improving

Training is the best way to improve racial/ethnic diversity in an organization. This might seem cliché, but it works.

In terms of communication, employees need training to develop empathy and understanding of the differences between their coworkers. This breaks down invisible barriers and encourages collaboration that improves job performance.

Training also improves workplace integration. Employees can be taught that they need to work with coworkers who are different to learn, grow, and progress within the organization. This opens the door to the exchanging of ideas and knowledge and helps the organization achieve goals and objectives.

If D'Andre and Juan undergo some type of training, then they will learn to leave their comfort zones and discuss workplace happenings with each other. This will benefit them and the organization as they share ideas and learn more about their jobs.

In summary, racial/ethnic diversity in organizations involves Asians, Blacks, Latinos (Hispanics), Native Americans, and Whites who are linked together by physical characteristics, nationality, and culture. This type of diversity is beneficial because it promotes unique and innovative thinking, but it also divides employees and keeps them from leaving their comfort zones. Training is the best method to overcome the challenges involved with racial/ethnic diversity because it teaches people how to interact, transfer information, and learn more about the work they perform.

Religious Diversity

This type of diversity is based on people's religious affiliations. Examples include Christianity, Islam, Judaism, and Buddhism...but this is by no means an exhaustive list, and sub-religions fall within each major category. A conservative estimate is that there are more than 1000 religious denominations in the United States.

In organizations, religious diversity refers to the variety of religions found in the workplace. This diversity might seem insignificant at first glance, but it actually drives change in the workforce...especially as companies compete in the global marketplace and employ people from different cultures all over the world.

Another reason religion has entered the workplace is that faith and spirituality are no longer restricted to employees' private lives. They take their religion to work with them, express it freely, and even let it define them as people. In fact, some people consider religion to be the most important aspect of their lives and would not work at an organization that does not respect their spirituality. This is in sharp contrast to the not-so-distant past when religion had no place in corporate America.

In short, employees with many different religious beliefs work together every day to accomplish objectives established by their organizations. Their spirituality affects their perception of the workplace and the way they are perceived by others. These variances lead to disagreements about best business practices regarding faith, and so far there has not been a perfect resolution to the problem.

Please consider the following concerning religious diversity in organizations:

Benefits

Religious diversity allows employees to express their freedom in the workplace. Their spiritual beliefs cannot be controlled, and this is particularly satisfying in a place where performance is measured and activities are monitored on a regular basis.

Religious diversity also promotes peace in organizations. Religion is very important to some employees, and they become upset is their spiritual faith is disrespected. This can lead to workplace conflicts and disruption that hinder productivity. Tolerance and acceptance of religious diversity reduce hostility and conflict because people feel respected.

Most importantly, religious diversity in organizations promotes trust in management. This trust leads to increased morale and retention of valuable personnel. Additionally, employees who trust leadership will work harder to achieve the objectives established by the organization, and this positively impacts the bottom line.

Organizational example

Haleema works as a cashier at a grocery store. She is Muslim and wears a facial scarf as part of her religion. The owner of the grocery store respects Haleema's religious beliefs and encourages her to wear the scarf as she services customers.

The owner's respect motivates Haleema to work hard every day. She truly believes that the grocery store is a good organization and strives to be the best cashier possible.

Ultimately, Haleema trusts the owner due to his acceptance and support of her religious values. This increases her morale, inspires her to work harder, and positively impacts the grocery store's bottom line.

Challenges

Religious diversity is beneficial in many workplaces, but it also faces some challenges that can be upsetting to some employees.

One challenge involves organizations with religious overtones. Some owners try to push their personal religious beliefs on their employees, and this can be offensive to workers who are not of the same faith or are non-religious. Some employees might not even want to participate in celebrations for religious holidays such as Christmas.

Another challenge is the fact that paid holidays are geared towards specific religions. For instance, employees get paid for Easter which is celebrated by many Christian denominations, but they do not get paid for Greek Easter which is celebrated by the Greek Orthodox faith.

Organizational example

Bernie is a Jewish purchasing agent at a paper mill. He has been with the company for seven years and is thought of as a very good employee by coworkers and management.

Bernie asks to schedule off two days to celebrate Rosh Hashanah, also know known as the Jewish New Year. His employer denies his request because Rosh Hashanah occurs at a busy time for the paper mill, and they do not recognize the Jewish New Year as a holiday.

This denial infuriates Bernie because he has strong ties to the Jewish faith, and he believes it is being disrespected by management at the paper mill. Based on this, he decides to quit his job because he considers his faith to be more important.

In short, management at the paper mill recognizes religious holidays for some employees, but not for others. Bernie feels disrespected and reacts by quitting his job. As a result of religious intolerance, the company loses a valuable employee.

Improving

There are actually many ways to improve religious diversity in the workplace. The following are a few ideas that work, but they might be impractical for some organizations:

- Organizations should implement policies regarding prayer and practice of religious observances. For instance, a room could be provided for employees to use for religious purposes. This meets the religious needs of employees and builds a positive relationship with management.

- Organizations should be aware of all religious holidays and try to avoid scheduling important events during those times. For example, they should not schedule a mandatory meeting for all employees on a known religious holiday. This is considered disrespectful and insensitive by affected employees. Along the same lines, organizations should honor requests of people who request time off for religious reasons. In the example involving Bernie, the paper mill should have approved his time off. This would have made him happy and prevented him from leaving the company.

Here are some ideas that can be implemented in any workplace:

- Organizations should plan celebrations that do not exclude any employees. Consideration should be given to the choice of decorations, speeches, prayers, and entertainment. For example, the company "Christmas party" could be changed to the company "holiday party," and the theme could focus on happy holidays instead of merry Christmas.

- Organizations should encourage employees of different religious backgrounds to interact and work together. This helps them learn about each other, and it acts as a catalyst for accepting different behavior. For example, teams can be assembled with religiously diverse members. The common goal of finding solutions to problems inspires members to work closely with each other.

In summary, religious diversity occurs in most organizations. It is beneficial because it promotes freedom, peace, and trust, but it also faces challenges due to disrespect and lack of tolerance. The best way to overcome these challenges is to make accommodations for religious practices, become aware of religious holidays, include all religions in celebrations, and encourage interaction between employees with different faiths.

Summary

Workplace diversity is not always understood because it involves unfamiliar customs and cultures from a wide variety of different people. Regardless of the understanding involved, it needs to be respected for people to work together and successfully achieve organizational goals and objectives.

This book examines and discusses the concept of diversity in organizations, the four major types of diversity in organizations (age, gender, racial/ethnic, and religious), the challenges involved with the four major types of diversity in organizations, and the best ways to improve the four major types of diversity in organizations. Workplace examples are used for clarification in every section, and academic jargon is avoided to make learning easier.

Congratulations! You now have a better understanding of diversity in organizations.

Stereotyping in Organizations
Problems and Solutions

Louis Bevoc

Published by
NutriNiche Systems LLC

Louis Bevoc books...simple explanations of complex subjects

Introduction

Stereotyping is a social psychological phenomenon found almost everywhere in the world. It occurs when people place others in specific categories and make assumptions and generalizations about the way they behave. These assumptions and generalizations are not necessarily accurate, but they are often thought of as facts based on personal beliefs or experiences.

Stereotyping can be positive or negative. Negative stereotypes are derogatory, often focusing on characteristics such as ethnicity, gender, age, race, religion, or sexual orientation. An example is the thinking that a woman cannot be a referee in the National Football League (NFL). This is not justified because she does not have to compete against the giant men who play the game. She only needs to make sure that they abide by the rules and penalize them if they do not. Positive stereotypes usually focus on specific groups of people. An example is the thinking that all Asians are good at math. Again, this is not true, and it puts unnecessary pressure to meet certain mathematical standards on Asians who find the subject challenging.

Employees often categorize coworkers for purposes of organizing. They separate people based on perceived differences, and this helps them better understand their workplaces. Unfortunately, this categorizing is done with little or no information about the people being grouped together. In short, employees are stereotyped based on perceptions rather than their contributions to the organization.

People's perception of others is their reality, but that reality is not always factual. For example, introverted people are not necessarily shy. They simply might not be interested in talking to everyone they meet, or they feel they learn more by listening than they do by speaking. Along the same lines, people who seem rude might actually be shy, librarians are not always boring, and owner's children are not necessarily spoiled brats.

We need to remember that our coworkers differ in a variety of ways besides the obvious race, gender, and age. Other factors such as religion, marital status, introversion, extroversion, position, and outside interests make them unique. Stereotyping them based on these differences can lead to workplace problems that are often difficult to resolve.

We will discuss the negative effects of stereotyping later, but first, let's look at some examples of how employees categorize each other in the workplace.

Examples of stereotyping in organizations

When employees stereotype coworkers, they make assumptions. Subconsciously, they try to confirm those assumptions and might actually witness a limited number of supporting incidents. This reinforces their beliefs about the stereotype, and it becomes even more difficult to disregard.

While some stereotypes are unique, others are fairly common. Below are characteristics associated with typical workplace stereotypes and examples of employees who use those characteristics in ways that are not normally associated with the stereotypes.

Accountant stereotype

These professionals are responsible for money in organizations. They are conservative individuals who lack creativity, and they have very little flexibility with the rules they abide by. Accounts prefer things to be structured and in order. Lack of structure upsets them, and they impose strict guidelines on coworkers to avoid it.

Non-conforming example

Jenna is an accountant for an automotive manufacturer. She loves cars, and that is why she chose to work in the automobile industry. Specifically, she likes fast cars and competes in amateur stock car racing on the weekends. Stock car racing interests her because there are explicit rules for the physical construction of the cars that are allowed to race. Essentially, every racer drives the same basic automobile, so mental ability and sharpness rank above all else in the quest for victory. Jenna's understanding of numbers allows her to calculate her average time and speed during every race for a competitive edge. Her knowledge of auto racing rules and regulations is also excellent, and because of this, she has been asked to be part of a board that establishes policies and procedures for future competitions.

IT stereotype

These people are introverted nerds. They enjoy working independently, prefer not to socialize with others, and the conversations they take part in usually involve technical jargon. Essentially, their lives revolve around computer-based technology.

Non-conforming example

Shawn is an IT person for a chain of Mexican-style restaurants. He keeps the corporate computer system operating, and he can fix just about any hardware or software problem he encounters. His technical knowledge also comes in handy for his side projects. He plays guitar in a psychedelic rock band and is able to produce desired sounds by using amplifier-based software that he created. He also developed a computer-based light show program that he sells to other musicians for use in their stage shows. Because Shawn prefers to think things through, he gives the appearance of being introverted. He enjoys working independently and this is why he creates new software for his interests. He also likes playing guitar because he can do this without the help of others. His life revolves around computer technology, and it helps him pursue his interests.

Salesperson stereotype

These individuals are pushy and willing to do anything for a sale. They do not care if the company makes money as long as they receive a commission check. In short, their concern is for their own well-being rather than their coworkers.

Non-conforming example

Rhonda sells life and health insurance for a national insurance company. She is aggressive in her job and works hard toward making a sale. Part of her aggression, however, involves making sure she gets a fair price for the product she sells. She wants to earn a commission, but she also wants to make sure the company is profitable so she can continue working there until she retires. In short, she thinks about herself and the company while she is on the job.

Young and single with no children stereotype

These folks are self-centered and more interested in their social life than their job. They do not have time or commitment worries because they don't have a family to be concerned about, so they can stay out late doing whatever interests them.

Non-conforming example

Nathan works for a furniture brokerage firm as a buyer. He is a young man with no wife or children. He does not have to be home for family responsibilities, so he can spend time doing whatever interests him. In Nathan's case, however, his job is his major interest. He works late trying to impress management with the goals he accomplishes. Much of his social life revolves around his coworkers, and they often discuss their jobs when they go out at night. Jason is very company oriented, and his parents and friends know it.

Mother stereotype

These women work for a second income. Their paychecks supplement their husband's wages, so it is not critical that they remain in the workforce. Mothers are not committed to their jobs because their families come first, and that will never change.

Non-conforming example

Margaret is employed as a Vice President of a bank. She works to provide a second income, but that income is necessary because her husband makes far less money than she does. Since her family needs her paycheck to maintain their lifestyle, she is very committed to her job. Yes, Margaret's primary concern is her family. That family, however, needs to be provided for monetarily...and Margaret's job allows her to be the provider.

Father stereotype

These men are the major source of income for their families. They work as late as necessary because their wives are the primary caregivers for their children. Fathers are very committed to their jobs because they have freedom from most family responsibilities.

Non-conforming example

Dennis is the receiving manager in a party supply warehouse. He works late to finish his job, and his wife is out of the state all week for her pharmaceutical sales position. Dennis' wife cannot quit her job because she is the major wage earner in the family, and Dennis needs to work because they need to save for retirement and college for three children. Dennis goes directly home after work to take care of his children and relieve his mother-in-law of her babysitting responsibility. Dennis works hard, and he is also a dedicated family man.

The above examples show that employees need to keep an open mind about their coworkers. People need to be viewed as individuals rather than members of classified categories. This starts by avoiding the temptation to make assumptions about others, and it leads us to the next section on the reasons behind organizational stereotyping.

Reasons for stereotyping in organizations

Stereotyping has gone on for centuries and likely will go on well into the future. The fact that this happens is not surprising, but it does raise a question. Why do people commonly stereotype others? Below are three major reasons.

Significance

People learn to categorize others based on significant influences in their lives. Those influences include family (parents, grandparents, aunts, uncles, siblings, etc.), teachers, coaches, bosses, coworkers, friends, and the media. Essentially, they listen to people that they respect or admire and accept their beliefs and opinions as fact.

Organizational Example

Jack is the owner of a water bottling facility. He tells Tracy, a QC technician, that all IT employees are geeks. Tracy believes Jack since he has achieved success in the business world, and now she considers all IT people to be nerds. Jack is a significant person to Tracy, so she accepted his stereotyping of IT people.

Sense-making

People have an inherent need to place others into groups that make sense. Once this is done, they no longer need to look at each individual when trying to process information. Instead, they look at the entire group and make a generic analysis thereby saving time and effort. Predictions about the future can also be made based on the information they have available about the stereotype.

Organizational Example

Wanda is a supervisor in a noodle manufacturing company. She has hired hundreds of people in the past, and her experience allows her to make decisions based on their appearance. If they are young males, then she has them work in the back of the plant because she assumes they can handle the heavy lifting. If they are young females, then she has them work in the packaging department because she assumes they are nimble with their hands. If they are people over the age of 40, she has them work in the retail section because she assumes they know how to interact with people. Classification of employees makes sense to Wanda because it allows her to facilitate the process of putting them to work. However, it also results in unfair stereotyping because not every person fits into her pre-designated categories.

Comparison

People like to place themselves and others in groups that can be used as social measurement tools. They compare their group to other groups and conclude which one is better. Bias is often present here because people favor the group that they put themselves in. This is similar to a person favoring their own hometown professional baseball team because they feel a part of it.

Organizational Example

Robert is a chemist in a laboratory. He tends to speak of the entire staff of chemists as a group when he talks about his job. For instance, he said, "we ran 20 different tests on the gas spectrometer for that customer." He also groups other scientists together. For example, he said, "the microbiologists were unable to find any viruses in the hospital's surgery rooms." These classifications allow Robert to compare his work group to other work groups in the company, but they also result in stereotypes that every individual does not fit into.

Now that you understand some of the basic reasons employees are stereotyped, let's move on to the effects of these generalizations after people experience them.

Effects of stereotyping in organizations

Stereotyping in organizations is harmful. It labels people based on limited knowledge and facts, and this is not fair to the individuals being classified. For example, consider a "mad scientist." A person who is skilled in scientific research does not necessarily live his life with a disheveled appearance while completely oblivious to his surroundings. This might be the case in some instances, but it is insulting to scientists who don't fit the description.

Some negative effects of stereotyping in organizations are fairly common. Below are typical issues that result from workplace stereotypes and examples of employees who experience the negative impact.

Self-fulfilling prophecy issues

Strange as it might sound, stereotyped workers sometimes behave in ways expected of them by those creating the stereotyping...even if that behavior was never real to begin with. This behavior might be forced upon them by others who are looking for reasons to categorize them, or it may be self-inflicted due to being around the stereotype for so long. Regardless of why this happens, delusions about stereotyping may influence some individuals to fulfill once false prophecies. This is not good because it reinforces stereotypes and makes people believe their generalizations and categorizations are based on facts rather than perception.

Organizational example

Andrea is the owner of a small GPS device manufacturer, and she is falsely rumored to be experiencing severe issues with her personal finances. Her vendors have experienced problems with companies whose owners were in financial trouble in the past, and they are nervous. They begin making Andrea pay cash for the parts she purchases. This affects her cash flow, and she has to withdraw money from her personal bank account until it is empty. Now Andrea cannot buy the parts she needs to manufacture her GPS devices. Her customers can't get product, so they start buying GPS devices from other companies. Andrea's sales decline, she shuts down her business, and she is forced to declare personal bankruptcy. She has fulfilled the once-false prophecy.

Cultural issues

In this situation, stereotyped people are not utilized to their full potential. Management does not make use of their established skills, nor do they let them develop new skills for use in the future. Quite simply, they are not given opportunities based on pre-conceived notions about their abilities. This negatively affects motivation, creativity, and productivity, and it can result in employees leaving the organization.

Organizational example

Hyun is an Asian immigrant who recently became an American citizen. He works as a computer programmer and does his job very well. Charles, his boss, knows Hyun has great technological abilities, but he views him as lacking the necessary communication skills to meet customers on sales calls. Because of this, Charles rarely lets Hyun leave the building for outside visits. This demoralizes Hyun. He knows he needs to work on his language and communication skills, but he cannot do this if Charles does not let him visit customers. Eventually, Hyun takes a position at another company. He left his old job because he was not given opportunities to acquire new skills based on a stereotype about his abilities.

Self-worth issues

Some people see themselves as more valuable than they actually are to an organization based on the perception they have of others. Their view of other employees is condescending because they see their accomplishments as more important...even though this is not always true. In fact, in some cases, the opposite is actually reality, and this causes problems within the organization.

Organizational example

Caitlyn works as an editor for a magazine. She has an English degree from a reputable university, and this is her first job out of college. Most of the other editors on staff are at least 20 years older than Caitlyn. They do not have college educations, but they do have a lot of experience. Caitlyn looks down on the editors who have not gone to college. She equates her academic credentials with success as an editor even though she lacks the knowledge of the rest of the staff. In reality, the older editors have experience that makes them more valuable to the magazine. Caitlyn's arrogance causes conflict with the other editors. They do not like her and she dislikes them. The end result is a decrease in efficiency and productivity of the entire staff.

Cooperation issues

People who make assumptions about others often put up an imaginary barrier that is difficult to penetrate. They avoid working with others they perceive as different because they assume there will be conflict and disagreement. This thinking is based on pre-conceived notions, not facts, and it leads to a lack of communication and lower productivity. The worst part about this type of problem is that it can easily be prevented if people make an honest effort to get to each other for who they are instead of the group they are classified within.

Organizational example

Stacy and Donald are both nurses at a doctor's office. Donald is an avid hunter, and Stacy is an animal rights activist. Donald does not want to work with Stacy, and he avoids talking to her on lunch and breaks because he fears she will attack him for his hunting interest. This avoidance leads to problems because the two nurses need to communicate with each other about certain situations regarding patients and that communication is severely hindered. Unfortunately, this issue is entirely due to misunderstanding. Donald is unaware that Stacy is not against hunting. She is an animal rights activist, but her only goal is to prevent the mistreatment of pets that people bring into their homes. If Donald made an effort to get to know Stacy, there would not be a problem.

Expectation issues

This problem typically occurs when employees make positive generalizations about others. It involves false impressions that certain people are capable of solving problems or resolving issues outside of their area of expertise simply because they are good at their job. Expectation issues create unnecessary pressure on the people being asked for help because they do not want to fail or disappoint those seeking their advice.

Organizational example

Katie works as a consultant for an environmental company. She has a Ph.D. in biology and is quite knowledgeable in her field. Her knowledge has earned her respect within the company, and because of this people often come to her for advice. Today George needs help with his 401K, and he asks Katie where she thinks he should invest his money. Katie is not a financial advisor, and she is afraid to make recommendations because George might become upset if her choices do not perform well. Katie is under pressure to help a coworker in an area where she lacks expertise. Because she has a Ph.D. and is good at her job, George assumes that she has knowledge about investing. George is positively stereotyping Katie, and that Stereotype is not accurate.

Other issues

Unfortunately, stereotyping can result in a variety of other negative issues. It produces employee stress, absenteeism, and turnover...all of which can impact performance to a point where the affected employee is no longer valuable to the organization. This sometimes occurs when management tries to hire people with pre-designated values, physical characteristics, or affiliations.

Organizational example

Patty has worked as a stewardess in a small airline for the past month. Her boss, Melanie, hired her on the recommendation of a work acquaintance, but things are not going smoothly. It's obvious that Melanie prefers young, tall, and slender stewardesses on fights. Patty is short with an athletic build, and she feels like she is being micromanaged. She becomes stressed over the situation, and this leads to her feeling ill. She does not want to lose her job, so she sees a doctor who tells her to take time off due to mental fatigue. While Patty is off on sick leave, she is of little value to the airline, and it reinforces Melanie's belief that stewardesses need to fit into a certain category.

Based on the examples above, it is clear that categorizing employees creates problems in organizations. Now that we understand the negative effects of stereotyping in the workplace, let's move on to methods of prevention.

Preventing stereotyping in organizations

People are the most important aspect of the organizations that employ them. Those people lose motivation and become less productive when they are stereotyped, and they might even leave their jobs if the cultures remain unchanged.

Leadership is responsible for preventing stereotyping in organizations because they establish the culture. They set the tone for behavioral standards using written and unwritten procedures. Below are some ideas that can be implemented by management to prevent stereotyping from becoming a destructive force.

Maintain awareness

Leadership needs to continually look for stereotyping that might be going on within their organization. This can be done by measuring attitudes, communication, trust, and respect using qualitative methodology (surveys) or quantitative methodology (open-ended questionnaires). Results reveal (1) employee perceptions of the organization and (2) employee thoughts on changes that could be made to make everyone feel more included.

Organizational example

Management at Henderson Controls conducts bi-yearly cultural audits in their facilities. These audits examine characteristics of culture including norms, values, and assumptions. The results indicate the existence of stereotyping and can be used to find the root cause of the problem. When the cause is discovered, Henderson's leadership implements changes designed to eliminate it and prevent future occurrences. These changes include employee suggestions that help prevent workers from feeling excluded as the organization moves towards achieving its goals.

Implement policies

Policies are important because they establish guidelines and provide direction for employees so they understand exactly what is considered acceptable and unacceptable behavior. These written protocols cite basic anti-discrimination laws enforced by agencies such as the United States EEOC (Equal Employment Opportunity Commission). In short, policies make employees think twice before stereotyping their coworkers.

Organizational example

Harper Plastics develops policies and posts them at the time clock and in the employee break room. These policies provide guidelines for treating people fairly by not subjecting them to classifications. They also cite laws implemented by the EEOC that specifically prevent workplace stereotyping and harassment. The policies are designed to prevent complaints regarding stereotyping by making employees aware of their legal and ethical responsibilities.

Incorporate training

Training can be used to help employees understand the need for making their workplace free of stereotypes. Lectures, role-playing, motivational speeches, videos, and question-and-answer sessions can all be used to explore employee generalizations in terms of work style, age difference, ethnicity, and ethics. These programs are developed by experts who have many years of experience in stereotype prevention, and their experience greatly increases the chance of success for the people being trained.

Organizational example

The CEO at Eccentric Guitar and Drum makes diversity training available to all employees. An outside company that specializes in diversity-related issues is hired to conduct the training using lectures, videos, and role-playing. This training focuses on age differences and work styles since some employees create instruments while others assemble them, and their ages range from 18 to 64. The training is designed to help employees understand each other's behavioral differences and move toward a stereotype-free workplace.

Reassign work

This idea helps generate understanding about people who are different, and it reduces false beliefs that working with those people is challenging. In short, it changes employees' normal routines by having them work with people they have rarely or never worked with in the past. Exposure to diverse types of people reduces pre-conceived prejudices and stereotypes as relationships develop.

Organizational example

Jerry Reed and Robert Schubering, co-founders of Reed & Schubering Distribution, implement a work reassignment program for their 250 employees. At first, the employees resist the change because they are removed from their comfort zones. However, over time they get to know workers from other parts of the facility and realize that those employees are hard-working people who are dedicated to their jobs. This prevents stereotyping in the company because employees have a better understanding of each other and don't generalize based on appearance or job classification.

Rotate Jobs

This process helps people establish empathy for the work others do at their jobs. Essentially, employees "walk a mile in other employees' shoes" by doing their job for a designated period of time. This prevents stereotyping because employees no longer falsely assume the details of their coworker's job's since they have done the work themselves. As an added benefit, people form relationships with each other as they discuss the jobs that they have done.

Organizational example

Palomino Landscaping is one of the biggest landscaping companies in the Midwest. They employ over 1100 people and want to avoid problems with stereotyping due to their diverse workforce. Management has begun to implement job sharing so employees develop empathy for each other's jobs and refrain from stereotyping each other. This program succeeds as employees gain a better understanding of the work performed by others. Stereotyping is now being prevented, and management is very happy. They realize the company is growing at a rapid pace, and false generalizations from employees about their co-workers could lead to major issues...including lawsuits.

Essentially, the best way to avoid stereotyping in organizations is to incorporate solid prevention plans that are designed and implemented by leadership or experienced professionals. These plans need written policies that are derived from employee input, and they should include training that helps employees develop empathy by understanding each other personally and professionally.

Summary

This book discusses people in organizations who place their coworkers in specific categories for significance (influence of important people), comparison (to other groups), or sense-making (for ease of processing information) purposes. These classifications are rarely based on fact, but they are thought of as the truth by many employees.

The importance of stereotyping in organizations is also discussed. Stereotyped people are exemplified, negative effects are noted, and prevention strategies are touched upon. This leads to a better understanding of why employees should not classify coworkers using pre-conceived notions. The problems that result from this type of behavior can lead to much more serious issues, and stereotypes are difficult to eradicate once they begin. Since it is difficult to eliminate false generalizations once they are rooted in the culture, the best way to avoid them is to implement prevention strategies.

Favoritism in Organizations

Types, Effects, and Options for Change

Louis Bevoc

Published by
NutriNiche System LLC

Louis Bevoc books...simple explanations of complex subjects

Introduction

Favoritism is typically not a good thing because it is often perceived as unfair. Consider the following definition:

> Favoritism is the act of providing privileged treatment to certain people at the expense of others.

Workplace favoritism occurs all over the world. It's there, it's real, it's difficult to eliminate, and it can lead to a variety of problems. People often get upset when unqualified coworkers are promoted to higher positions based on the relationships they have with those in power. This can lead to decreased morale and poor attitudes that negatively impact the entire organization, and it can be so bad that employees look elsewhere for employment.

Most favoritism in organizations is legal, even though it might be considered wrong or unethical by some people. For example, if the owner of a company likes someone and chooses to promote that individual, then there is no legal way to prevent it. However, if that promotion is based solely on the exchange of sexual favors, then it is illegal and it can be prevented.

This book examines different types of favoritism in organizations (friends, family, relationships, and linkage). Next, it then looks at the effects favoritism has on employees' loyalty, motivation, morale, and attitude. Then it moves into options employees have for change after experiencing favoritism including doing nothing, staying and fighting, or leaving the organization. Last, but not least, it examines the future of workplace favoritism.

Please note that the legal aspects of workplace favoritism will not be discussed. The focus of this book is to simply describe and exemplify the types that exist in organizations.

Now that you have a basic understanding of what this book entails, let's move into the specific types of favoritism.

Types

Favoritism is a fairly broad term, but it can be broken down into categories for better understanding. The following are some specific types of favoritism along with workplace examples for illustration purposes:

Friends

This involves hiring, promoting, or giving special treatment to friends regardless of their qualifications. Also known as cronyism, this type of favoritism goes on in organizations all over the world, and it causes a lot of problems. Employees find it difficult to accept the special treatment of unqualified coworkers just because they have established friendships with those in charge.

Organizational example

Orlando has worked for a commercial fishing company for the past seven years. He has good working relationships with the customers, and the owner Brian has made him second in command.

Currently, Brian serves as captain of the ship. However, he recently announces that he is stepping down from this position to focus on other aspects of the business. Orlando is fairly certain that he will be offered the captain's job until Brian unexpectedly announces that he is giving it to a man he has been friends with for over 20 years.

Brian's choice of a new captain is very upsetting to Orlando. In fact, he is so upset that he begins to look for a new job. He's not sure exactly where he wants to work, but he feels he cannot work for Brian any longer.

Orlando is a dedicated employee who found it insulting that the owner of the shipping vessel did not promote him to captain. He is so upset, that he starts searching for different employment...and it is all due to favoritism involving friends.

Family

This involves hiring, promoting, or giving special treatment to family members regardless of their qualifications. In family businesses, this favoritism, also known as nepotism, is quite common. It is also understandable when owners have worked hard to build a company. They want their children to take over the businesses that they have founded and established. Additionally, some siblings are more than qualified to take over their parent's business. A daughter, for example, might earn an MBA from a prestigious business school and work for several years in many different facets of the organization. She gradually takes leadership of the company in small chunks, learning as she moves forward. This, combined with the fact that her father is the best mentor available for learning, makes her a good fit for the CEO position when she eventually moves into it.

While nepotism in organizations can work out well, there are also consequences with this type of favoritism...and unfortunately, this applies to the majority of situations. Loyal or long-term employees get discouraged when they see the "kid" with no experience or qualifications move into a position that he or she has not earned.

An even bigger problem with family favoritism involves uncles, aunts, brothers, sisters, cousins, and other family members. Employees find it very upsetting when a key job is given to a brother or sister who has no experience, qualifications, or birthright.

Organizational example

James has worked for a car dealership for the past 19 years, and he has worked his way up to the assistant general manager position. He is very loyal to the company, and the owner Jerry has great respect for him.

Two years ago, the owner of the dealership's daughter Rachelle graduated from college and began working at the dealership. She started out in sales and has moved around the dealership to work in almost every department for short periods of time to learn the business.

The general manager of the dealership is retiring next year, and Jerry announces that his daughter Rachelle will be taking over the position. This is somewhat demoralizing to James since he has worked hard for the company, but he does understand that Jerry wants the position to go to his daughter.

James is a long-term employee who is discouraged since he believes he is the most qualified for the general manager position, but also he understands that Jerry wants his daughter to take over the business. This workplace favoritism was a direct result of Rachelle being part of the family.

Relationship

This involves hiring, promoting, or giving special treatment to boyfriends, girlfriends, mistresses, or someone else with sexual or emotional ties regardless of their qualifications. It causes problems because people believe the person getting the special treatment has not earned it. Additionally, the emotions involved in these types of situations create other issues. Individuals receiving special treatment might influence the people in power due to loving or sexual relationships with them. In fact, people in power can be so influenced that they make decisions that are best for their partner rather than the organization. This not only upsets employees, but it also jeopardizes the well-being of the organization.

Organizational example

Tammy is a secretary at an electrical supply company. She has worked for the company for two years, but she has more influence on the owner Chuck's business decisions than any other employee. The reason for this is that she is Chuck's girlfriend.

Tammy is disdained by many of the other employees at the electrical supplier. They believe she lacks business skills, and they are upset that she is involved in major decisions regarding the direction of the company.

The worst part about this situation is that the other employees feel like they work for Tammy instead of Chuck. When she tells them to do something, they believe they must comply or risk getting in trouble with Chuck. Additionally, their actions are monitored by Tammy, and she reports them to Chuck if she does not approve.

Tammy's position and authority damage the moral and motivation of the entire workforce, and it is all due to relationship favoritism.

Linkage

This is an indirect type of favoritism, and typically friends and family are the beneficiaries. It involves putting qualified and trusted individuals into important positions and then asking them for personal favors down the line. It is somewhat sneaky and deceptive, and it is also unethical in certain situations.

Organizational example

Cindy is the president of a large plastic injection molding company. In her position, she is allowed to appoint two members to the board of directors. She recently appointed Jonathon to one of the board positions.

Jonathon is easily qualified to be a board member since he has been the president of two different injection molders in the past. However, Cindy has an ulterior motive for her appointment. She wants Jonathon to hire two of her friends into important positions within the company. She does not want to do this herself because it would look like favoritism to friends, so she uses Jonathon to accomplish the task.

Cindy does not want to appear as if she is favoring her friends, so she appoints someone qualified and trusted to do the work for her. This action is a direct result of linkage favoritism.

Now you understand the different types of favoritism that occur in organizations. You can also see that they have negative effects on other employees. The next section will discuss those effects in more detail.

Effects

Many people have witnessed some form of favoritism in the workplace, especially in terms of promotions. This is often not considered fair, but it is reality and problems do result.

The most interesting fact about favoritism in organizations is that many leaders believe they have policies and procedures in place to combat it. However, there are always ways to get around the rules...especially for those who are in power. Employees typically will not argue with decisions made by higher-up managers for fear of jeopardizing their own jobs.

This section examines the effects of favoritism. Unfortunately, the vast majority of those effects are negative, so the negatives will be the major focus. Workplace examples will also be used for better understanding. Please consider the following effects:

Motivation

Employee motivation evolves from people's feelings about work. It is the psychological force that determines their behavior within the organization, and it affects their persistence, drive, and effort.

Demotivated employees lose interest in their jobs. They are frustrated, tend to spend a good deal of their time complaining, and absenteeism is sometimes an issue. This type of behavior results in a lack of productivity, and the bottom line is negatively impacted. In short, the way employees feel about themselves and their jobs directly affect their drive to achieve the goals and objectives of the organization.

Employees are demotivated when they feel that they are being treated unfairly. If they see coworkers treated in special ways, they feel resentment and hostility. Favoritism opens the floodgates to demotivation, and any employee who has experienced it knows the feeling firsthand.

Organizational example

Mickey has worked in a retail store for the past six years. He is currently the manager of the men's department, does a very good job, and has a strong desire to continue to grow with the organization.

Mickey has just been informed that the assistant manager position in the store is open. He is the most qualified employee for the job based on his work experience, so he expects to get the promotion. However, a job offer never comes because the store manager promotes Jenny, a friend of his, to the position. Jenny has been with the company for less than two years, and she was only a lead worker in the cosmetics department before the promotion.

Jenny's promotion is very demotivating to Mickey. He dedicated six years of his life to the retail store, and now he is passed over for a job he believes he truly deserved. He loses interest in his job and begins to call in sick because he does not feel like going to work. This impacts the bottom line of the store because it is less efficient when Mickey is absent.

Mickey lost his desire to work because he personally experienced a coworker getting special treatment due to her friendship with someone in power. His lack of motivation negatively impacted the company, and it was due to favoritism in the organization.

Morale

Employee morale is defined as the outlook employees have about their workplace. It involves their thoughts about the work they perform and their overall job satisfaction.

Favoritism often results in a lack of recognition, and a lack of recognition is one sure way to lower employee morale. When employees' morale is lowered, their drive to achieve organizational goals decreases, and their job satisfaction diminishes.

Organizational example

Veronica works is an assistant office manager at an optometry center with five different doctors. She has been with the company for six years and performs her job very well. She is organized and efficient, and she gets along with all of the doctors and patients. She also strives to make the organization the best that it can be.

The office manager is retiring in one month, and Veronica is the obvious choice for the job. However, without warning, it is announced that the daughter of one of the doctors is going to be given the position. This is very demoralizing to Veronica since she is much more qualified and deserving than the doctor's daughter. Her job satisfaction comes to a crashing halt, and she has a very negative outlook on her employer. She is no longer concerned about the best interests of the company because she feels the organization did not reward her for her efforts.

Veronica did not feel she was properly recognized for her efforts, and this led to a decrease in her morale. This problem was a direct result of favoritism in the organization.

Attitude

Employee attitudes influence their responses to different types of stimuli. In other words, their attitude predisposes them to respond positively or negatively to situations or ideas.

Favoritism in organizations can result in bad attitudes and cause people to respond negatively to ideas or situations. When this happens, employees are characterized as negative by others and this starts a downward spiral for their careers. There is truth to the adage, "attitude determines altitude" in the workplace.

Organizational example

Andrew is an accountant at a telephone service company. He has worked for the organization for nine years, is typically upbeat and happy, and is well-liked by management and coworkers.

The president of the company announces that the controller's position is now open because the current controller Sarah is retiring. Andrew applies for this job, but it is ultimately given to another accountant who has less experience than Andrew, but is a personal friend of Sarah and the president.

Andrew is upset that he was passed over for the controller's position, and it shows in his attitude. Coworkers frequently hear him saying that he does not care what happens in the organization, and he no longer seems happy at work. This is a big difference from the way he was before he was passed over for the promotion.

Andrews's disappointment about not getting the controller's position shows in his negative attitude, and it is a direct result of his perception of workplace favoritism.

Loyalty

Loyalty is a feeling of commitment or support towards someone or something. In workplaces, this means feeling committed to the goals of the organization. When people experience favoritism, they often become less loyal to the organization. Unfortunately, this might be the worst negative effect of favoritism because people who lose loyalty often look for other employment.

Organizational example

Allison has worked as a website designer at an advertising agency for the past three years. She is very dedicated to the organization and believes in accomplishing its objectives. She has no problem working late at the office or from home on the weekends because she wants to grow with the company.

Allison's goal is to use her technical background to get into sales at the advertising agency. The president announces that a sales position is now open due to an employee leaving the organization. Allison applies for this job and wants it badly, but it is ultimately given to the son of the vice president.

Allison is dejected after getting passed over for the sales position. The man selected for the job was much less qualified than her, and he only received it because he was related to someone in power. She starts leaving the office earlier on weekdays and no longer works from home on the weekends. She is also considering looking for other employment.

Allison's loyalty was drastically reduced because she was passed up for a promotion that she thought she deserved, and it all resulted from favoritism at the advertising agency.

Now you understand some of the negative effects of favoritism in the workplace. This leads to a question. What can be done after you had a bad experience with favoritism? This question will be explored in the next section.

Options for Change

What can be done after you have a bad experience with workplace favoritism? That is a good question, but basically, you have three options. These options are as follows:

Do nothing

This is the easiest option because it requires the least amount of effort. Employees do not have to do anything except continue on with the organization. They can learn to be satisfied with their current position, or they can hope for some type of improvement/advancement at a later date. Employees who prefer to avoid conflict might select this type of response to favoritism.

The disadvantage of this option is that it can be the least satisfying. Employees who do nothing might end up holding a grudge. This is not good for the employee or the organization, and the grudge could turn permanent as the employee thinks about what happened.

> **Note:** It might always be best to choose this option at first to reassess the situation. Are you overlooking something important? For example, was the promotion given to the other employee for a reason that you are not seeing? Was that person actually qualified in ways that you are not aware of? The answer to these questions might all be "no," but you owe it to yourself and the organization to think about every possible explanation. After all, your response to this perceived favoritism could potentially impact your career.

Organizational example

Susan works as an inventory control supervisor at a grocery store chain warehouse. She started with the organization seven years ago after she graduated from college, has been promoted to a management position, and has received excellent reviews every year.

Susan finds out that the director of inventory control is leaving the company, and that position is now available. She immediately applies for the job and believes she has a very good shot at getting it. However, it is soon announced that Nathan from the purchasing department has been given the job. This upsets Susan because Nathan has less inventory control experience than she does, and he has not worked in her department for more than ten years.

Susan is demoralized over not getting the job, but she decides she is going to remain in her current position without complaining. After a few days, she settles down and begins to think about what happened. Nathan has over 20 years of experience with the company. He is an experienced purchasing agent and has worked closely with the inventory control people for many years. He also worked in inventory control for six years before taking a job in purchasing.

Susan's rethinking makes her realize that Nathan was actually the best person for the position. He has a wealth of experience to offer the company, and his background is diverse. She is young and knows more opportunities will come along, so she decides to patiently wait for the next opportunity.

Susan chose to do nothing after the perceived favoritism. This ended up being a good choice because it allowed her time to rationalize why she was not given the promotion. After some thought, she understood the decision and chose to remain a loyal employee. In this case, doing nothing worked out well for the employee.

Stay and fight

This is the hardest option because it is difficult to fight powerful people in an organization...and where do employees begin? If possible, they should start with the manager who gave the special treatment to another individual. If the manager does not provide a sound explanation, then employees should go to their human resources department to attempt to find satisfaction.

> **Note:** This can be challenging in smaller companies that do not have human resource departments, but if this is the case then you should try to contact the owner. If the owner is the person who was responsible for the favoritism, then your only real choices are to do nothing or leave the organization.

> Additionally, if you choose to stay and fight, avoid emotional outbursts and personal attacks because they can lead to non-productive and destructive situations. If a discussion gets out of hand, it is very difficult to reach a compromise where everyone leaves with some sense of satisfaction.

Organizational example

Joseph is a technician at a laboratory that does a wide variety of chemical and microbiological testing. He has worked in the analytical chemistry department for over four years, and he is well-liked by management and coworkers.

Joseph's boss was recently promoted in the company, and this resulted in her job becoming vacant. Joseph applied for the position, but it was given to an employee in the microbiology department. This upsets Joseph because he truly felt that he deserved the job. He schedules a meeting with a vice president at the company and expresses his concern. The vice president does not give Joseph any satisfaction, so he schedules a meeting with the human resources director Melanie. Melanie cannot help him with this situation, but she promises that she will talk to upper management about him, and he will seriously be considered for the next lab manager position that comes available.

Joseph finds some satisfaction after talking to Melanie. He likes his job, but he wants to progress within the organization and is willing to fight to achieve that progression.

Leave the organization

This is usually a last-resort option. Some employees simply cannot sit back and do nothing, so they try to stay and fight. However, their fighting is in vain because they do not find satisfaction in talking to management or human resources. Employees who cannot come to terms with the favoritism might be better off being employed elsewhere.

> **Note:** In almost every situation, it is ill-advised to quit on the spot. This burns bridges and those bridges might be needed down the line. Make sure you have another position lined up, and give the customary two-week notice. You will be much more respected if you handle your resignation professionally.

Organizational example

Candice works for a uniform company as a delivery/warehouse person. She has done this job for five years, and the is well-liked by coworkers and customers. A supervisory position at the warehouse opens up, and Candice applies for it. She has wanted this job since she started working for the company, and she believes she is the most qualified employee based on her experience.

Candice finds out that the position was given to the wife of the owner's son. This is very demoralizing to her because she was passed up for a position that she feels she deserved. Worse yet, the position was filled by a person with no related experience simply because that person had ties to the owner's family. After some serious thought, Candice decides to look for employment elsewhere. Within six weeks, she gives a two-week notice to work for a competitor in a similar position.

Candice could not come to terms with the favoritism she experienced, and she did not see anything from preventing this from happening again. She felt she had no other choice but to leave the organization. However, she did not quit on the spot. She acted professionally by finding other employment and giving proper notice of resignation.

Now you are aware of the options you have after you experience workplace favoritism. These might not resolve the situation completely, but they can offer some sense of satisfaction.

It's rather obvious that workplace favoritism has a major impact on people's careers, and this is not likely to change. That being said, let's explore the future of this phenomenon.

Future

Unfortunately, favoritism in the workplace will likely go on as long as there are organizations. People want to help others they care about, and this is easily accomplished when those wishing to provide aid are in positions of power.

So what does this mean? It means you need to be prepared to deal with favoritism. Be ready to apply your options for change when you work for any organization. Remember the old saying, "failing to plan is planning to fail."

Additionally, if you are in a position of power, try to think about the impact on other employees before you make a decision based on favoritism. How will it affect them? Will they lose motivation or develop bad attitudes? Will it cause internal conflicts? Will important employees leave the organization? These are all important questions to consider, and the answers can prevent you from losing the respect of your coworkers and subordinates.

Summary

The significance of workplace favoritism cannot be underestimated. It creates a variety of employee problems and can be very destructive to organizations. On rare occasions, favoritism produces good results, but typically the negatives outweigh the positives.

This book explores favoritism in organizations. First, it examines specific types involving friends, family, relationships, and linkages. Next, it looks at motivation, morale, attitude, and loyalty to see how these factors are affected. Then it moves into options for change that include doing nothing, staying and fighting, and leaving the organization. Last, but not least, it explores the future of the phenomenon.

Congratulations! You now understand workplace favoritism...a significant aspect of organizational behavior.

Nepotism
in Organizations
Understanding and Surviving

Louis Bevoc

Published by
NutriNiche System LLC

Louis Bevoc books...simple explanations of complex subjects

Introduction to nepotism

This book is about nepotism in organizations. It explores the concept in workplaces from an employee and employer perspective.

Let's begin by asking a few questions:

What is nepotism?

Nepotism is showing favoritism to relatives. Interestingly, it originated in the Catholic Church. Popes, like many business people in higher positions, wanted family members to benefit from their achievements. Since they typically did not have children due to their vow of chastity, popes selected their nephews for bishop and cardinal positions. This was not always fair to people who were more qualified and devoted to the church, but it was reality...and that same type of reality exists in many organizations today.

In workplaces, nepotism is favoritism toward relatives for special treatment within organizations. This special treatment can involve job titles, promotions, compensation, recognition, awards...and just about anything else that is construed as positive and typically needs to be earned.

The problem with nepotism in organizations is that many relatives who benefit have not earned the privilege. They are rewarded due to "who they are" rather than "what they have achieved." This has consequences because oftentimes more qualified workers are passed over simply because they are not related to those in charge.

Is nepotism discrimination?

Yes, nepotism is a form of workplace discrimination, but it is not necessarily illegal. Laws prevent discrimination for reasons including nationality, race, religion, disabilities, or gender. However, there is no law to prevent nepotism...especially if the benefiting employee is qualified.

What determines qualified?

This is a very good question, and sometimes the answer involves controversial or shady business practices. There are many ways to determine the meaning of qualified.

Consider the following methods of determination that can be manipulated for reasons involving nepotism:

Knowledge and skills

> Employees often get jobs based on their knowledge or skills. However, management establishes the required knowledge and skills, and they can alter them to suit specific needs. This is not uncommon in cases involving nepotism.

For example, assume a manufacturing engineer and an industrial psychologist both work for an automotive manufacturing plant. The engineer has worked in the manufacturing area of the plant for ten years improving processes and troubleshooting problems. The industrial psychologist has worked in the offices of the plant for ten years researching the communication climate of the organization.

The president of the company creates a job is created for an assistant plant manager, and it interests the engineer and the psychologist. It's rather obvious that the engineer is more qualified than the psychologist for the job because he understands manufacturing much better. However, the psychologist is the brother of the president, and the president wants him to get the job.

To make the selection of the psychologist appear fair, the president makes an advanced degree in social sciences, communication, or psychology a requirement for the position. The reasoning behind this is that the assistant plant manager will be expected to understand people using his or her education and training.

The psychologist is given the position because the engineer's master's degree is in business. This seems unfair, but there is little that can be done about it because the psychologist was better qualified based on the job specifications.

In this case, nepotism changed the job requirements. The president wanted his brother to get the position, so the job specifications were tailored toward a psychologist's qualifications.

- **Testing**

Tests are a way to determine qualifications for jobs. Candidates answer job-related questions and those who score the highest are given preference for the position.

Testing is a legitimate means of determining qualified candidates. However, nepotism can change this process in a way that makes it illegitimate. This is done by providing relatives with the answers to questions in advance. The relatives then get high test scores, and they are awarded the positions.

Providing relatives with test answers in advance is unjust and illegal, but nobody usually finds out...so the relative is given the job without incident or objection. Unfortunately, this favoritism provides a good example of how nepotism results in unfair treatment of employees.

- **New position**

Sometimes new positions are created in organizations. In fact, this is quite common as organizations grow. However, there are also times when newly created positions are specifically designed for relatives. This serves a dual purpose. First, it allows relatives to have good jobs. Second, it avoids the discontent that results when employees are passed up for positions that already exist.

An example of a new position created by management is a special projects manager. What are a special projects manager's responsibilities? This is a good question because those responsibilities can entail just about anything...from taking out the trash to running an important project. The obvious purpose of this job is to give the relative a good position within the organization. It's not illegal, but sometimes it borders on being unethical.

- **Education**

  Specific education can be made mandatory for certain jobs. This is a reasonable policy because organizations want employees to have specified training before they take on a job. However, education can be manipulated for nepotism purposes. For example, a master's degree in liberal arts might be a requirement for an upper-management marketing position. Not surprisingly, the owner's daughter might be the only employee who meets this qualification. This is somewhat shady, but it skirts around some of the legal issues that could potentially surface.

- **Seniority**

  This is one of the least common ways to promote or reward people through nepotism, but it works in certain situations. For example, a relative who has no skills or education might have the most seniority in the department or company. That seniority can then be used to promote this individual without fear of legal action based on discrimination. This type of promotion can be particularly demoralizing to other employees if the relative being promoted has a history of poor job performance, but remained employed due to being a family member.

What does this mean?

It means that nepotism can and does occur in many organizations...and there is little that can be legally done about it. Employees in high positions want their relatives to get the best jobs in the organization, and they will do whatever is necessary to make sure this happens.

The above answers indicate nepotism causes problems in organizations, and we will discuss those problems in more detail in the *Reasons nepotism is bad* section of this book. However, not all nepotism is bad, and the next section explores some of the positives of this type of favoritism.

Reasons nepotism is good

As noted above (and will be discussed later in this book), nepotism causes issues in workplaces. It borders on being shady or unethical in some situations, but it usually avoids falling into the category of illegal. However, in some instances, nepotism makes sense. In other instances, nepotism is beneficial to the organization.

The following are some reasons why nepotism makes sense or is beneficial to organizations:

- *Birthright*

  Understandably, owners want their children to take over the organizations that they have founded and established. These entrepreneurs have worked hard to build businesses, and they want their offspring to benefit from their efforts...regardless of the opinions of other employees. Handing the reins over to future generations might not necessarily be beneficial for organizations, but it makes sense because owners have the right to decide who will run their companies.

- *Qualifications*

  Nepotism is often associated with negative thoughts because it gives special treatment to undeserving relatives. However, this is not always the case. Sometimes relatives are the most qualified people for prestigious jobs, and that is why those jobs are awarded to them. In this case, the relative and the organization benefit.

- *Commitment*

  Family members are often more committed to the goals and objectives of the workplace than other employees. Sometimes this is due to the fact they have ownership in the organization, but it also results because family members feel an emotional attachment. The success or failure of the organization is a direct reflection of family, and for this reason, they want to see it succeed.

- *Loyalty*

  Loyalty is a feeling of commitment or support towards someone or something. In workplaces, this means feeling committed to the goals of the organization. Family members are often very loyal to their place of work. They remain with the organization regardless of the circumstances because they feel they should do so. Unfortunately, family members are sometimes loyal to a fault because certain circumstances dictate they should sell the business or shut it down.

- *Trust*

  Relatives have more trust in each other than they do in complete strangers. This applies at home and work, and it is one of the reasons workplaces use nepotism for filling important positions. There is truth in the old saying, "if you can't trust your family, then who can you trust?"

- *Turnover*

  Relatives often believe they have an opportunity or play a major role in the organization. Even if they do not establish ownership, they have a good chance of achieving a position of importance. Because of this, their turnover is lower than other employees.

The above reasons show why nepotism has legitimacy in organizations, and they can be combined to make promotions of relatives even more legitimate.

The following example combines birthright and qualifications:

> Charles has been employed by a car dealership for the past 15 years, and he has worked his way up to the assistant general manager position. He is very loyal to the company, and the owner Ted has great respect for him.
>
> Five years ago, Ted's daughter Angela graduated from college and began working at the dealership. She started out in sales and has moved around the dealership to work in almost every department for short periods of time to learn the business.
>
> The general manager of the dealership is retiring next year, and Ted announces that his daughter Angela will be taking over the position. This is somewhat demoralizing to Charles since he has worked hard for the company, but he does understand that Ted wants the position to go to his daughter.
>
> Charles is a long-term employee who is the most qualified for the general manager position, but he understands that Ted wants his daughter to take over the business.

In short, nepotism has some good reasons for existing in workplaces. However, as noted earlier, it also has some bad reasons for being utilized...and those reasons are discussed in the next section.

Reasons nepotism is bad

Nepotism works out well in some organizations, but there are also consequences with this type of favoritism...and unfortunately, this applies to the majority of situations. Loyal or long-term employees get discouraged when they see the "kid" with no experience or qualifications move into a position that he or she has not earned.

The following are some specific reasons why nepotism is not good for organizations:

- *Favoritism*

    Favoritism is the act of providing privileged treatment to certain people at the expense of others. Employees who experience nepotism in the workplace see favoritism given to relatives and find it upsetting. While this favoritism might be legal, it is considered wrong or unethical by many workers, and this creates discontent and other problems.

- *Morale*

    Employee morale is defined as the outlook employees have about their workplace. It involves their thoughts about the work they perform and their overall job satisfaction. Nepotism lowers morale because employees perceive it as unfair. When morale is lowered, employees lose their drive to achieve organizational goals, and their job satisfaction diminishes.

- *Attitude*

Employee attitudes influence their responses to different types of stimuli. In other words, their attitude predisposes them to respond positively or negatively to situations or ideas. Nepotism results in bad attitudes and causes workers to respond negatively to ideas or situations. When this happens, those employees are characterized as negative by others and this starts a downward spiral for their careers. There is truth to the adage, "attitude determines altitude" in the workplace.

- *Work responsibilities*

This problem results when family members shift their responsibilities to other workers in the organization. These privileged individuals prefer to "oversee operations" rather than perform specific tasks, and other workers are forced to take on those tasks. Unfortunately, there is little that these workers can do because they do not have the authority or power to refuse the additional work. In short, some family members' responsibilities diminish as they are added to other employees' workloads.

- *Discipline*

This presents a big challenge for employees. It is very hard for non-family members to discipline family members because, in reality, those family members are not held responsible for their actions.

A good example of this is a young man starting work at his father's company after graduation from college. This young man knows nothing about his dad's business, but he is free to get involved with any aspect of it. When he does something wrong, managers cannot discipline him because his only real boss is his father. Managers know that the owner's son will mostly be able to do as he pleases, and they do not want to jeopardize their own jobs by trying to control him. This means the son is left to behave as he chooses, and this causes many problems in the workplace.

- *Honesty*

Employees are afraid to be honest about relatives for fear they might upset those in power...and this is a legitimate fear.

For example, assume an employee named John witnesses the CEO's niece sleeping at work. He tells the CEO about what he has seen, but the CEO becomes upset and accuses John of "unfairly" attacking his niece. Instead of reprimanding his niece, the CEO transfers John to another department. This action sends a message to the other employees that they should never be honest about any negative behavior of family members...or they will face consequences.

- *Power struggles*

Power struggles due to nepotism occur when different employees try to control the activities and direction of the organization. They do not agree on everything, and the arguments that result create a variety of workplace problems. Not surprisingly, non-family employees bear the brunt of these issues.

Two different types of workplace power struggles include:

Family members fighting with each other

This occurs when members of the same family fight over power in the organization. For example, a son and a daughter both want to be in charge of their father's company. They make decisions without consulting each other, and this causes problems because conflicting signals are sent to the employees and customers. The tension between the two siblings is felt by everyone, and the situation creates an ugly mess as the battle rages.

This situation is unfair to the employees because they are unsure of the direction of the company. It is also wrong because the workers are caught in the middle of a conflict that should be handled by the owner. Unfortunately, this type of sibling rivalry is not uncommon in small businesses because owners do not want to side with one child, and they believe their children will eventually resolve the problems themselves.

Owners fighting with each other

Another type of power struggle involves organizations where there are multiple owners with different families. A partnership fits this category, but another example is a corporation where two people have equal ownership. If both owners bring in family members, then major problems can result as warring factions are established in the workplace. When the owners start arguing over the positions and power of the various family members, they lose sight of the goals of the business and instead focus on their personal objectives. This type of power struggle can cause chaos in an organization...and destroy it in the process.

The above reasons show why nepotism is not good for organizations. Many problems result when this type of favoritism is shown, and the consequences can have a negative impact on the workplace.

You are now aware of some of the negative aspects involved with workplace nepotism. Based on these, it might appear difficult to work in organizations where family members are in charge. However, this is not always the case. In fact, many people do quite well working in environments laden with nepotism. They do this by learning to survive...and those survival techniques are discussed in the next section.

Surviving nepotism

Employees who find themselves in workplaces with nepotism are not necessarily in a bad position. In fact, if they do things right, they can have very rewarding and successful careers. The key to this success is learning to adapt to the environment. This adaption is no different than it is in other workplaces...except for the fact that family members' traits and idiosyncrasies are involved.

The following are guidelines for surviving in workplaces with nepotism:

- *Be realistic*

  Employees working in family-owned businesses need to understand that the owners' children are likely going to get good positions in that organization. As noted earlier in this book, these owners work hard to establish their businesses, and they want their children to benefit from their efforts.

  Nepotism does not guarantee the kids will run their parent's businesses, but it does mean that they will likely have it easier than other employees as long as their parents remain owners. This is the way it was in the past, the way it is now, and the way it will be in the future. Non-family employees need to accept this reality and do their best to find happiness in their current situation, or they can look for employment with another organization that is not family-owned.

- *Be objective*

  Employees should try to view workplaces with nepotism as if they were the owner or CEO. What would they do? Would they make similar decisions? They might be surprised to discover that they would think along the same lines if they were in charge.

  Objective thinking likely will not change the situation, but it will change employees' views of that situation. This makes things better due to a different perception. Everyone has a perception...and that perception truly is their reality.

- *Focus on the positives*

  Negativity rarely works in a job situation...and this includes workplaces with nepotism. Employees need to stay as upbeat as possible. They need to focus on the positive aspects of their jobs. For example, if the owner of a company did a good job, then his daughter might do the same. After all, the apple typically doesn't fall far from the tree.

  Additionally, nepotism typically occurs in small businesses where it is easier to form relationships with the relatives in charge. This is advantageous for many reasons including recognition for jobs well done. Employees in larger organizations are often considered "spokes in the wheel," and they do not stand out for their individual accomplishments. Over time, recognition by family members for good work leads to rewards...including pay raises and bonuses.

- *Avoid gossip*

This guideline is much more significant than it might appear to be at first glance. It is important to not get involved with any type of gossip about family members in the organization because there will be consequences if they find out. Gossipers are viewed by family members as employees that cannot be trusted. That lack of trust can prevent raises, bonuses, promotions, and job assignments that involve confidentiality...and it can stop a career in a heartbeat. The worst part about losing trust is that it is difficult to restore once it is gone.

- *Avoid adversity*

Never conspire to work against family members. Employees are much better off attempting to befriend all relatives rather than taking sides with a select few. This sometimes involves walking a tightrope, but it can be done. Employees who stay neutral during power struggles are much more likely to survive when those struggles are resolved.

- *Discuss concerns*

Employees who feel comfortable with leadership in organizations can take their concerns to the top. However, this needs to be done diplomatically. Never attack family members directly, and only focus on matters that concern those in change. Talk about the fact that nepotism is affecting the company's bottom line because leaders are concerned about profitability. Also, discuss how the actions of family members are perceived by customers because customers are critical for organizational survival. In short, avoid discussing negatives about relatives and instead focus on the effects of their actions on the organization.

- *Suggest policy changes*

When meeting with leadership, employees can also suggest policy changes that minimize the negative effects of nepotism. These suggestions include incorporating:

1. A policy that immediate family members do not work in the same department. This minimizes some of the power struggles that occur when family members are responsible for the same tasks.
2. A policy that family members do not directly supervise each other. This minimizes workplace arguments that occur when one relative feels mistreated by another.
3. A policy that discussions between management and employees will be kept confidential. This diminishes the fear of retaliation by family members if complaints are lodged against them.

Policy changes can make a difference in workplaces with nepotism. They prevent problems by avoiding situations where they are most likely to occur.

Summary

Nepotism occurs in workplaces all over the world, and it will likely go on as long as leaders have family members that want good jobs. It produces some negative effects, but it is also justifiable in many situations.

This book focuses on nepotism in organizations. It answers the following questions:

- How is nepotism good for organizations?
- How is nepotism bad for organizations?
- How do employees survive nepotism in organizations?

Simple explanations are used for answering these questions, and workplace examples are incorporated for better understanding.

Congratulations! You now understand more about nepotism in workplaces...an important aspect of organizational behavior.